40 HOUR MAN

by
Stephen Beaupre
and
Steve Lafler

MANX MEDIA

ISBN #0-9769690-0-9

13 digit ISBN #978-0-9769690-0-6

Comics and Graphic Novels

Library of Congress Control Number: 2005937546

ON THE CLOCK

What do you do? We all know the question. It's the boilerplate social setting ice-breaker. Unless you want to be seen as a dolt, you'd better have an answer ready. Ideally a tidy encapsulation of your purpose in life, defined by what you're currently willing to do for money. Are you a plumber, a dental hygienist, an Office of Homeland Security library card fetishist? What you do is what you are. If you doubt that, check any obituary headline. Vern Plotkin, 88, Insurance Adjuster. Vern also loved to play the bongos. But that detail gets lost when insurance needs to be adjusted.

I've always dreaded the ol' "what do you do?" When I was in a blue-collar orbit, I didn't want to be defined by my crappy job du jour. Once I shed my steel toe shoes, I was more concerned that someone might find my line of work to be of interest and actually want to talk about it! I realize not everyone shares the same short circuit when it comes to this topic. But still, I wonder about this thing we call work. Is it truly life-defining? Or is it simply a means to an end (high definition television) and nothing more? Moreover, how do we know the difference?

Needless to say there are BIG QUESTIONS swirling around the meaning of work in our lives. But don't worry. This book pretty much avoids all of that deep-thought head-scratching. Instead, I've decided to try to disarm the ticking "what do you do" time bomb once and for all by expounding upon every job I've ever had, in strict chronological order, until you run screaming from the room. Is it therapy? Entertainment? Torture? You bet!

This madness has to be seen to be believed. Words alone simply won't suffice. Thankfully, cartoonist-extraordinaire Steve Lafler is in charge of the VISUAL IMPACT portion of our journey. It's harmonic convergence of the first order. Steve and I have been friends for over thirty years (gak!), roughly the same time period covered by this book, and he plays a key role in many of these stories. Blend in the fact that he's fashioned a career as an artist without joining the 9-to-5 world, and you have an extra layer of subtext that could only be plotted by NASA. Be-Bop Tango!

You can't fire me — I quit!

ON THE CLOCK (CONT.)

Stephen Beaupre and I have been friends for more than thirty years; we are two 20th century models pushing forward into the new millennium with our deeply ingrained, well-earned bad attitudes.

Sharing an instinctive lack of respect for authority and a willingness to test the limits of any hierarchy within kicking range, Mr. Beaupre and I are the perfect pair of malcontents to take on a project like *40 Hour Man*, our humorous deconstruction of the workaday world.

For my own part, I'd say the path to such satirical hijinks was paved by Harvey Kurtzman, the man with the audacity to take on the straight laced conventions of the Fifties, creating *Mad* magazine. With impossibly witty artists like Will Elder and Jack Davis carrying out his vision, Harvey set a high water mark for gag filled comics in the satirical vein.

By the time I got to *Mad* at age 12, in 1969, Harvey was long since gone from the masthead, but the "Usual gang of idiots" aptly carried out Kurtzman's mission to poke fun at any convention and/or sacred cow they got their hands on. For me, my involvement in *40 Hour Man* is one big long love note to you, Harvey!

And to my pal Mr. Beaupre; I found working on this piece to be an experience in friendship on a telepathic level. As I drew, I had every confidence that I was carrying out Steve's vision (It doesn't hurt that we were born four months apart, virtually into the same cultural milieu). From start to finish, it's been nothing but a rockin' good time.

STEVE LAFLER

You're gonna wind up working in a gas station.

— Frank Zappa

Pretty good pants.

— Art, the Grill Chef

1

STUPID
BLUE SMOCK

Have you ever stopped to consider all the jobs you've had? Taken one at a time, each one almost makes sense. String them together and the plot crumbles. We're trained to call it a career, but that's just smoke and marketing. Let's face it — unless you're a trust fund baby, a Saudi prince, or Willie Nelson, work is doing the thing you don't want to do, to make money to do the thing you do want to do. Only there's no time, because you gotta go to work. Let me start at the beginning.

I caught a glimpse of the work-gratification scam years before I encountered my first real job. I just didn't realize it at the time. I was twelve years old and my summer "job" was selling cheap address labels door-to-door. I did it so I could "win" a camera and "earn" a school trip to Washington, DC. It was humiliating. But my neighbors felt sorry for me and bought the labels they didn't need, so I could stop doing the thing I didn't want to do, and get what I thought I wanted. Go, capitalism!

A fast-forward four years later I found myself at the customary labor-induction age of sixteen. The free ride was officially over. While the details are unclear, I somehow applied for, and landed, a part-time job at a drugstore chain called MediMart. It was there, amongst the lip balm, shampoo and cherry cough syrup, that I was introduced to the Zen-like purity to be found in limited responsibility and low wages. I was a stock clerk. I wore a blue smock. I was a total dork.

The four-hour shifts seemed endless. It was as if I had discovered a whole new way of parceling out and measuring time. Each shift was basically the same: I stocked and neatened the shelves and took orders from the assistant manager (a lowly retail species located just above Tilt-a-Whirl operator on the career choice chart). All stock boy activity was closely monitored by this poor unfortunate — everything from timing our twelve-minute breaks to instructing us in the fine art of sanitary napkin display.

My stint as a drugstore stooge ended rather abruptly. I'd been there just about four months when I was summoned to the manager's office, and without much fanfare informed that my services would no longer be required. I was shocked. As I slowly removed my stupid smock and stupid name tag, I meekly inquired into the reason behind my dismissal. "Basic incompetence," was the disinterested reply. My starting and finishing pay was a truly luxurious $1.85 an hour. (No, that's not a typo.)

On the rebound from my first firing (always a special time in a boy's life), I wound up at the Rustler Steakhouse, a cafeteria-style "Old West" restaurant that was set to open in the same strip mall as MediMart. They were still putting the finishing touches on the faux cowboy décor when I filled out my application. I was hired on the spot. Somehow I had managed to take my burgeoning flair for incompetence and move it two hundred yards to the left.

Before the night of the grand opening, all new employees (i.e., teenage miscreants) were required to attend an indoctrination session hosted by a perfectly-coifed district manager from the home office. The brainwashing consisted of a series of guidelines and philosophical tenets solemnly referred to as "The Rustler Way." It was a meat-based religion with a side of potato. When the sermon ended, they dimmed the lights and showed us an inspirational film featuring dancing T-bone steaks.

Now that I was sufficiently molded to their exacting corporate specifications, I was issued a horrid polyester cowboy suit, complete with poop-brown cowboy hat. Costume in hand, I was taken on a guided tour of my new work area. There would be no "front of the house" for me. I was relegated to the back of the restaurant — behind the main dining room (keep walking), behind the grill area (keep walking) — to an area known as "the pit." This was my office. I was the dishwasher.

I was quite pleased with my assignment. In the pit I would
have little or no contact with the beef-happy public; that
was left to the waitresses and the busboys. Plus, since I
was safely out of sight, I was spared the indignity of having to wear the silly cowboy hat. But freedom comes with
a price. My price was standing in a three-foot-square area,
force-feeding an endless parade of mushroom gravy en-
crusted dishware into the hot dripping steel mouth of the
industrial dishwashing beast.

All night long busboys trooped into the pit with trays of dirty dishes, slamming the trays on the conveyer belt that led to my command center. One of the busboys was a funny, red-haired kid named Steve (illustrious illustrator of this very tale). We were both equipped with an appreciation of the absurd and could quote Frank Zappa with conviction. We became fast friends and from that point on we endeavored to transform the nightly drudgery into something more to our liking.

It wasn't long before we were going out drinking after work. The drinking age was eighteen at the time, and we were barely seventeen, but we didn't let a little technicality like that stop us. Our watering hole of choice was The Gin Mill, a delightful snake pit that was also the favorite hangout of a local motorcycle gang called The Huns. It's hard to fathom now, but we used to sit there in our cowboy costumes drinking beers, surrounded by angry three-hundred-pound bikers high on crystal meth.

Another notable busboy from the steakhouse era was Rich, a likable sort with a penchant for ingesting large amounts of whatever illegal chemical crossed his path. Rich lived near me, so we'd occasionally give each other a ride to work. On one such commute, he offered me a small white pill he called "cannebanal" (see "elephant tranquilizer"). He said, "I just took one, you should too." It seemed perfectly logical to me at the time, so I took him up on his offer.

The mystery drug worked its magic on our malleable brain matter. When we finally found our way to work (how, I have no idea), we were greeted by Mr. Dan, the dreaded (and on this occasion slightly glowing) assistant manager. He proclaimed that he had a very special assignment planned for us that evening. Great! He led us into the back room and presented us with brand new toothbrushes. Our job was to clean the cracks between the floor tiles.

The rest of the night was a bit of a blur. Reliable reports suggest we spent the next four hours down on our hands and knees, our faces two inches from the floor, furiously scrubbing away at the wavering tile mosaic. As the evening progressed, our collective mood would shift. We'd laugh hysterically for a while, then there would be an almost-contemplative period, followed by assorted barnyard noises. It was the best of times. It was the worst of times. It was minimum wage.

But all good things, even scrubbing the floor with a tooth-brush, must eventually come to an end. It wasn't long before management grew tired of Rich's prodigious drug consumption and inability to memorize the schedule, and gave him the boot. In a way, Rich was the sacrificial lamb. It could have been any of us. Every once in a while he'd wander into the restaurant and order a solitary baked po-tato. Just another forlorn figure slowly digesting the gar-nished tuber of rejection.

Instead of firing me, they cut my hours until I was down to one night a week. I loved the not-working part, but the no-money part was killing me. I was about to graduate from high school and had made plans with friends to rent a house at the beach that summer. I needed a short-term job to hold me over. That job turned out to be working at the Framingham Motor Inn, a faded no-frills motel overseen by a shadowy figure in a white linen suit who had a hook for a hand.

I was hired to wash dishes, but was liberated from kitchen duty by the maintenance supervisor, an easygoing character named Tony. All the maintenance guys loved working for Tony, and it was easy to see why. There wasn't much work involved. Each morning, he would round us up, hand out paintbrushes, and then vanish for the day. We responded to this honor policy like any other self-respecting group of punks: We went up on the roof and smoked dope.

The big project that summer was painting the motel pool, an Olympic-size monstrosity that hadn't been touched in decades. I'd like to say we rose to the challenge, but that's not quite right. Mostly we sat around in the deep end, paint scraper in one hand, beer in the other, keeping one eye out for Captain Hook. This could have been my life's work, but the beach was beckoning. My maintenance buddies were still in the pool when I left. For all I know, they are still down there.

2

POODLE HEAD
OF DESTINY

The master plan for the summer was to rent a house at the beach with a few of my high school compatriots. Perhaps "plan" is too strong a word. It sounded like a fun idea, so we did it. The day after I quit my maintenance gig, I packed up my trusty bong and black light posters and drove to Hampton Beach, New Hampshire, a decaying seaside resort town known for its pinball arcades, pervasive fried dough, and teenage girls in fringed halter tops.

My shallow cash reserves quickly forced me to rethink my standing as a beach bum. Before long I was taking a seat next to the other vagrants at the local unemployment agency. After filling out the necessary "teenage transient" forms and enduring a lecture on the importance of personal hygiene, I was set up with an interview at Whoopie Putt Mini Golf. I didn't know what to expect. But with the word "whoopie" in the name, how bad could it be?

If I was going to hang out at the beach all summer, I needed to land this job. To prepare for the interview, I traded
my t-shirt and jeans for a more acceptable "sport shirt and
slacks" combo. As a finishing touch, I stood in front of
the mirror and cut my shoulder-length hair until it achieved
the perfect Up with People look. Here I was, unemployed
for just two weeks and I was already willing to turn into a
Young Republican for the glory of minimum wage.

On the morning of the interview, I followed the directions to the home of Mr. and Mrs. Whoopie. I walked up to their modest beachfront bungalow and rang the doorbell. No answer. I rang it again. Nothing. As I was about to leave, a female specimen in a fuzzy bathrobe answered the door. I was struck (figuratively, literally, you name it) by her smudged red lipstick and industrial-strength perfume. She looked like she'd been in a bar fight and had just managed to make bail. She invited me in.

Chez Whoopie looked perfectly normal from the outside. But inside it was pure David Lynch deleted scene. As I glanced around the living room, I couldn't help but notice an amazing variety of poodle-related kitsch. It was everywhere. Embroidered poodle pillows, ceramic poodle lamps, oil-painted poodle portraiture ("In Loving Memory of Frenchie") and dozens of framed family photos, each featuring the same enormous poodle-dog. Arf, arf!

During the interview ("I'm relieved you're not one of those dirty hippies!"), Mrs. Whoopie smoked at least one hundred menthol cigarettes. There were always three or four half-finished smoldering butts in the ashtray when she would reach for a fresh one. Between the smoke fumes and poodle finery, I could barely concentrate on what she was saying. I just nodded my head. When it was over, she shook my hand and offered me the job. I couldn't get out of the house fast enough.

The job had a split-shift schedule. I'd work five hours in the morning, have time off in the afternoon, and then report back for more mini golf escapades in the evening. In theory, the split-shift equation sounded downright leisurely. In practice, it meant that I was never more than a few hours away from doing something that involved mini golf. The orange sun would be barely peeking over the fake windmill (hole #8) when I unlocked the front gate every morning.

An integral part of maintaining the aesthetic purity of the mini golf course involved the removal of the tiny pebbles that accumulated on its highly touted "Astro Turf Greens." I accomplished the eradication of these nefarious stones by strapping on a fifty-pound gas-fueled leaf blower device. It was a magnificently evil machine that belched thick black smoke from its snout-like hose and generated enough raw heat to cook a pot roast dinner on its exposed engine.

Once the greens were pristine, I'd retire to the confines of my office, a plywood hut about the size of an outhouse. From there, I could monitor the tourists as they whacked golf balls against the pink dinosaur (hole #12) and still perform my duties, which consisted mainly of handing out the tiny clubs, tiny pencils, tiny scorecards and other diminutive accessories associated with this form of fun. Get a hole-in-one in the clown's nose and win a free game!

After five hours of moving pebbles around and renting golf clubs to tourists, I was rewarded with an extended mid-day break. Early on, I imagined I'd use this free time for all sorts of new athletic pursuits. Heck, I was living at the beach — maybe I'd learn to surf! Instead, I found that I needed every minute of precious free time to forget what happened in the morning and steel myself for the evening shift. So I mostly drank beer on the beach. Surf's up!

When I'd check back in for the evening shift, Mr. and Mrs. Whoopie were making the scene, running the operation in their own ineffable fashion. In other words, they were reclining on beach chairs and tossing back frozen blender drinks. This was convenient, as I was also altered. After an exchange of slurred pleasantries, Mr. Whoopie would reach into the pocket of his madras shorts and hand me the keys to the big black Buick parked outside the gate.

Stretched out behind the Buick was a ten-foot trailer that supported an enormous plywood sign. The sign was adorned with a cartoon poodle head and the words "Let's All Whoopie Putt!" At the bottom of the sign was a pair of speakers which were connected to a microphone that was installed on the car's dashboard. My job was to haul this hallucination-in-progress up and down the beach's main drag, all the while testifying to the healing properties of mini golf.

Before I embarked on my maiden voyage, Mr. Whoopie gave me a script to read. But the canned speech got old quick. I was determined to make this interesting for my audience. After reciting the sanctioned sales pitch for a few laps, I'd switch to lounge singing and evangelical-style sermonizing. Needless to say this approach didn't go over too well with the owners. Most of the arguments we had that summer centered on reports they'd received about my nightly tour.

As fun as it was to yell whatever I wanted into the microphone, it was hard to keep up the amplified babbling for hours at a time. So I did sets. Whenever I ran low on inspiration, I would just turn up the car's radio and rest the microphone on the dashboard speaker. I distinctly recall the sight of old women clutching ice cream cones, running in horror from the advancing monster poodle head blaring "Purple Haze" from its civil defense-quality speakers.

On one occasion, while I was broadcasting an especially invigorating number for my public, Mrs. Whoopie pulled up alongside me in her massive red Cadillac. I happened to look to my left and there she was. Yikes! She rolled down the window of the Caddy, stuck her entire upper torso out the plush velour opening and screamed "I TOLD YOU, NO ROCK AND ROLL!" While the whole episode struck me as hilarious, it proved to be my final performance.

The next day when I arrived for work, I was greeted by a somber-looking Mr. Whoopie. He took me aside and explained that due to a slow summer (no doubt attributable to my daily pilfering of bills from the register), they could no longer afford to keep me on. There was no mention of how much his wife despised me. As I looked into his bloodshot eyes, I experienced a brief wave of empathy. I was being fired. He could never leave. I went out that night and celebrated my newfound freedom.

Hanging out at the beach had been big fun, but I still need-ed to bring in money to subsidize my lifestyle. My room-mates were just scraping by themselves and were in no position to pay my portion of the weekly rent. A young Albert Einstein once theorized "Income minus frequency equals outcome doubled." My personal outcome was swift eviction from my seaside bohemian love pad. I was fired and evicted all in one week. It was a personal best.

The weather was appropriately stormy on the morning I moved out of the beach house. It wasn't easy, but I managed to wedge every last one of my earthly possessions into my little green Pinto. I felt like a failed teenage pharaoh in a subcompact tomb. On the ride home it occurred to me that a crisply choreographed collision with a produce truck would erase all evidence of my existence. But the traffic was light that day and I moved back in with my parents.

Being back home after a brief fling with independence was like being strapped to the receiving end of an existential joy buzzer. There were still two months to go before college was scheduled to start and I desperately needed to replenish my finances. Also, my new favorite pastime — lounging around in my bathrobe while watching daytime television — was not going over well with the rest of the nuclear sitcom nest. It was time for a new game plan.

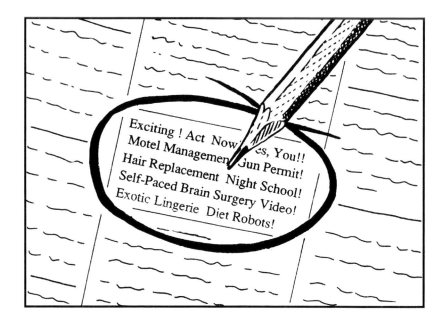

I began to scour the Help Wanted section of the daily news-paper, circling any ad that included the phrases "No Experi-ence Necessary," "Be Your Own Boss," or "Easy Money Now." These were the magic words specifically inserted to attract a certain class of job applicant. A bold person. A risk-taker. The type of person who would be willing to show up for a job interview and not care if he was be-ing sized up for corporate vice-president or monkey house bucket attendant. "Act Now!"

Swallowing what was left of my pride and beer, I dialed one of the circled ads at random. Waiting on the other end of the line was a gum-smacking operator straight out of central casting ("Irene" for the purpose of this tale). Much to my delight, Irene was not concerned about my job history, "skill set," or possible parole violations. Her mission was to schedule as many interviews as humanly possible. That was *her* meaningless job. I think I was #213.

47

The interview took place on the second floor of a down-town address that was also the home of Bumpy's Restaurant, a 50s-era breakfast spot known for its greasy eggs and greasy clientele. I was quite familiar with this particular historical landmark. Steve Lafler and I had been known to stop in there to sooth our teenage hangovers (too much screw-top apple wine) and take in the never-ending display of local color. Ah, Bumpy's. Meanwhile, upstairs . . .

The outer-office area was crowded with other lower-rung types. I glanced up and down the line and took inventory. Aimless drifter haunted by a checkered past? Check. Troubled loner mumbling in code? Check. Tattooed carny with a taste for the grape? Check. Downwardly mobile mini golf lackey? Yup. No one looked up as I took a seat. We sat there pretending to read the waiting room magazines; periodicals like "Industrial Solvent Monthly" and "Gear Bit Supplier."

I was halfway through an article on how to shop for a quality rubber apron when the office door creaked open and a mangled approximation of my name rang out. "Steve Boopee, please, Steve Booopeeee!" Once inside the inner sanctum, I was greeted by what appeared to be two reptilian envoys from a distant planet. It was quite unsettling. I didn't know whether to shake their bejeweled appendages or head for the nearest window and take my chances out on the ledge.

They took turns expounding on the money-making opportunities that were available to all those wise enough to sign up with their crusade. They reinforced the pitch with glossy pamphlets that pictured successful young androids relaxing on private yachts, surrounded by Norwegian fashion models wearing string bikinis. "People just like you, Mr. Booper!" My extremities were tingling. I felt like I was being subjected to a form of nightclub-level hypnotism.

The job was a commission-based form of sales enslavement wherein I wouldn't make a dime unless I moved truckloads of the "product." According to their master plan, I would patrol the mean streets making "cold call" visits to the homes of strangers. Once inside the domestic fortress, I would unveil the wonder product, at which point the housewife or unemployed longshoreman would throw themselves at my feet and turn over their life savings.

Sensing that they were close to losing me, one of the alien beings ceremoniously produced a red velvet case. It was time to reveal the item that held the power to make all our dreams come true. I leaned in. He slowly opened the lid. I looked inside. It was . . . steak knives. They wanted me to sell steak knives door-to-door. "Honey, there's a stranger at the door with a box of knives and he wants come in." I was still laughing when they led me out of the office.

Freed from the clutches of the knife gang, I moved on to the next help wanted ad. A local bakery warehouse was seeking an "On-Call Truck Handler." I was told they needed a few warm bodies who would be willing to come in on the third shift whenever someone called in sick or got crushed by a pallet of Twinkies. The big selling point, other than the enticing prospect of free baked goods, was that they were prepared to pay me a whopping $5.00 an hour.

It was a great job, until the first call came in at three o'clock on a Saturday morning. I had gone out that night with friends and was between REM and vegetative coma when the phone rang. I couldn't understand why the phone was ringing, or who the person was on the other end of the line. Unload trucks? Cupcakes? Apparently, "No fucking way!" was not the response they expected. It was the best I could muster on short notice. They never called back.

My next occupational entanglement is a bit of a mystery. All I remember is that I spent three weeks inside a carpet-cleaning cult called FiberShine. Like all good cults, FiberShine consisted of leaders and followers. In this case, the leaders were unpleasant management types in bad suits and the followers were the "Fiber Technicians," the poor souls who had to clean the carpets. Imagine a mix of Sears, Amway, and everything you've always suspected about Scientology.

Success and failure within the company was based on a Byzantine points system. Management earned points by putting the screws to the technicians, who in turn accumulated points by bilking the unsuspecting customers. Each morning, after an inspirational reading of the point totals, we would set forth in the company van, armed with industrial cleaning devices, vats of toxic chemicals, and a list of the people who had been foolish enough to request a "free consultation."

The trick was to convince the customer/mark that every surface in their home needed immediate attention — the carpeting, upholstery, bedding, everything! We were told to use phrases like "irreparable damage" and "invisible lice" (my favorite). After hearing this, the victim would either grab a blunt object and chase us back to the van or go limp and take out the checkbook. After three weeks of this, my mind was the consistency of pudding. One morning I called in sick and never came back.

3

SPECTACULARLY UNFULFILLED

The summer of peace, love and futility had come and gone, and all I had to show for it was sand in my sneakers. Somehow I had managed to stagger from one dead-end job to another without saving one dime for college. After enduring a stirring rendition of "I told you so!" from my parents, I withdrew the $98.00 I had left in the bank and moved into a dorm room at Graham Junior College, a low-rent communications school that is now the site of a deep-dish pizza franchise.

I chose Graham because it was cheap and because the recruitment brochure listed Andy Kaufman as a graduate. What I didn't know was that the school was on the brink of financial collapse and the dorms were close to being condemned. On one memorable evening, I awoke to a commotion outside my room. When I opened the door, I witnessed my fellow residents, armed with hockey sticks, chasing rats down the hall. This was the extent of Graham's sports program.

I never held a real job while at school, unless you count
my Thursday night show on the college radio station. My
midnight shift was in perfect alignment with "Dime Beer
Night" at the school pub (this was the 70s, when drinking
was still a recognized contact sport). For two dollars (I'll
pause while you do the math), I could whip myself into a
stupor and still make it to the station in time to have Willie
Alexander's "Hit Her Wid De Ax" cued up on turntable one
by the stroke of twelve.

My next brush with employment took place during the summer after my freshman year. I had been home for two days when my friend Dave called and offered me an assistant cook/dishwasher gig at the nursing home owned by his parents. I believe the name of this particular retirement village was Shady Glen (or perhaps it was Musty Cave). As a further enticement, Dave told me that Pete, another friend of mine, had just been hired as the head cook.

I had no experience in the culinary arts, but that wasn't a problem. Pete and I would just grab a prefab "cutlet" or "puff" from the freezer and match it up with an industrial-size can of beans or creamed corn. The only exception was the daily bowl of spaghetti and red sauce we prepared for Tony, a loopy Italian resident who always wore a plaid pom-pom hat. If the spaghetti wasn't just right, Tony would storm into the kitchen and challenge us to a fight.

Each day, after I'd scrubbed the pans, I'd go out behind the building and have a smoke. As I sat out there on an old milk crate, I'd try to imagine what it would be like to have a job that I actually liked. Try as I might, I could only imagine the same paper hat and milk crate. One afternoon, Dave's dad caught me out back and asked me why I wasn't working. I told him that I had completed all of my chores. "Learn to work slower," he said. I turned in my apron and quit.

Since I was fresh out of prospects, I paid a visit to the local employment agency. It was like a bureaucratic spa treatment. You waited to fill out a form. You waited to turn in the form. You waited for your name to be called. The reward was an audience with a miserable state employee. This was the person who was going to find you a new job with a rewarding future. I never understood why they didn't take the good jobs themselves and get the hell out of there.

My sessions with these "employment consultants" were somewhat predictable. After a few preliminary questions related to my marketable skills (chuckle), job history (guffaw) and desired wages (wild laughter with gurgling sounds), they would stare into the void of the microfiche crystal ball and search for the right occupation to match my "profile." Eventually they would look up and say something like "Apprentice Wax Agitator, $5.10 to start?"

I actually went down to the wax factory to inquire about the agitator job. Despite all of the encouraging talk about vats of wax, rubber gloves and burn insurance, I neglected to put my real name on the application. Just as I was about to give up hope, I got a call from Steve Lafler. It seemed that he and our pal Rob had both been hired as security guards at an outfit known as Advance Security. Steve said they were looking for more able-bodied recruits.

I drove to Advance Security for a meeting with the man entrusted with the task of transforming delinquents like myself into steely security sentinels. That man was Ernie Stackpole. From the top of his crew cut head down to his brown wingtips, Ernie was a direct-from-central-casting drill sergeant gone to seed. I briefly worried that I might not have what it takes to be a security guard. Those fears proved to be unfounded. The first thing Ernie did was measure me for a uniform.

The uniform was a brown and white number with a big silver badge. I felt like I had been transported back to my Wild West steakhouse days. Only now I wasn't washing dishes. Now I was the damn sheriff! Ernie asked me if I was interested in carrying a gun on the job. He said I would be eligible for better assignments if I was packing some heat. I had only been there ten minutes and he wanted to give me a weapon to go with the brown pants. I declined.

My first gig was supposed to be at a department store in downtown Boston. But when I arrived, after a long subway ride in from the 'burbs, the store manager took one look at my Advance Security badge and told me to go home. Apparently, they'd just caught another Advance guard smoking dope in the ladies lingerie stockroom. Since there wasn't too much I could do in the city dressed like a cartoon cop, I hopped back on the subway and went home.

71

I called Ernie and told him what happened. He apologized
and assured me that the next assignment would be better.
He proceeded to give me directions to Steinman's Fine
Ladies Apparel in Roxbury, a Boston neighborhood with
a rich history and rising crime rate. The next day, I made
my way to the store and was introduced to the owner,
Mr. Saul Steinman. Saul was a diminutive, cardigan-clad
gentleman in his late fifties. He seemed very nervous and
very happy to see me.

Things had changed since Saul's father opened the store a generation ago. Back then, the neighborhood was upscale and most residents were Jewish. Now, many of the store-fronts were boarded up and the population was mostly poor and black. Saul told me to stand by the entrance. At one point, a group of teenage girls came in and taunted me. "You think we're gonna steal something!" I hadn't considered that. My effectiveness as a scarecrow was suspect.

It was the longest day of my life. After about six hours, I began to think that doing nothing might be more work than doing something. It seemed like a profound concept at the time. Maybe I was just hallucinating. As my shift was ending, Saul asked me to accompany him — guard him, I guess would be the idea — when he went to the bank to make the day's deposit. As we walked past tenement stoops crowded with unemployed men, I decided I would not be coming back.

My next assignment was a weekend gig at a trucking company. The truckers didn't work weekends, so it was just me and the trucks. This was better than Steinman's, but the reality was the same: I was getting paid to do nothing and nothing was a cruel mistress. One day I came across a rubber stamp that said "Driver Collect." Steve Lafler and I adopted that mystery directive as a euphemism for teenage love conquest. We even wrote a song in its honor.

The grand finale to my security guard career was a second shift detail at Polaroid. I was stationed in a sensory deprivation booth in the lobby that was just big enough for a chair and an impressive-looking security panel of blinking lights and toggle switches. Despite the aura of importance surrounding this prop, no one bothered to explain what it all meant. When an alarm went off, I would just flip switches until the siren stopped. This seemed to satisfy everyone.

I was supposed to check employee badges as people entered the building. That lasted about ten minutes. The way I figured it, the people coming and going had probably been working there for years. I had been in the booth for about an hour. It might have made more sense for them to ask to see my ID. Of course, the honor system was far from foolproof. Terrorists carrying briefcases brimming with plutonium could have walked by without causing a stir.

My afternoons in the booth were spent reading music magazines and composing anguished teenage poetry. After everyone had left for the day, I would conduct anthropological studies of the darkened office environs, transfixed by the pie charts and softball trophies. It amazed me that people would voluntarily spend eight hours a day in these carpeted holding cells. As a security guard, I was able to visit the scene of the crime without ever being the victim.

Inside the corporate jungle, the size of a person's chair is directly tied to the warrior's standing within the tribe. At this location, the largest and most luxurious swivel throne belonged to some guy named Ron, the vice president of marketing. It was a thing of beauty. Once the coast was clear, I would wheel his prized possession out onto the front steps of the building. From there, I could relax in style and watch the summer sun set behind the industrial park.

My shift ran from three in the afternoon until eleven at night. Since I was trapped there during the dinner hour, I'd bring along a sandwich to hold me over. On nights when I'd be meeting up with friends after work, I'd throw a cooler packed with beer into my car. When I got to the parking lot, I'd surreptitiously transfer the beer into a grocery bag and then — this part still amazes even me — I'd bring the bag filled with beer into the bustling office building.

I'd casually stroll past the various offices, my big clinking bag o' beer under one arm, until I reached the employee cafeteria. There, surrounded by executive-types on their afternoon break, I'd add my extra large lunch sack to the employee refrigerator, wedging it between the tuna fish sandwiches and containers of low fat yogurt. No one said a word. At this point I was not only getting paid to do nothing, I was getting paid to do nothing and drink beer. Clearly I was moving up the ladder.

My final night at Polaroid started out much like any other. The beers were chilling in the refrigerator and I was looking forward to going out after work. Steve Lafler and I had made plans to meet for drinks and miscellaneous mayhem at a local rock dungeon. Time was of the essence. I had finished all but one of my "work beers" and was waiting in my security booth for the next guard to show up and relieve me. Then the phone rang. It was Ernie Stackpole.

The guard who was supposed to relieve me had called in sick. Ernie now wanted me to work a double shift. I told him that there was no way I was going to stick around for another eight hours. (I was tired. I was almost out of beer!) Ernie responded with a sermon on the unique responsibility entrusted to those in the security profession. I listened to Ernie's spiel and hung up the phone. After about twenty seconds of soul-searching I decided to abandon ship.

I ran back to the cafeteria to grab my last beer. As I was closing the refrigerator, one of the night-shift janitors walked in holding a broom. Eureka! He couldn't speak English and my Spanish wasn't much better, but we both spoke the universal language of alcohol. I handed him the last cold bottle and gestured for him to follow me to the lobby. I showed him the security booth with its mysterious toggle switches and red lights. I pointed to the big chair on the front steps. Then I left.

Ernie called the next day and told me to turn in my uniform. I drove to the Advance headquarters and left it in
a bag outside of his office. (I kept the badge.) As I was
heading back to my car, I noticed a woman walking in
my direction. She looked to be in her mid-thirties and was
dressed like a secret agent from one of those Dean Martin
Matt Helm flicks: all dark sunglasses, tight white bellbot-
toms, high heels and hairspray. I didn't want to stare, but
I couldn't turn away.

She walked up to my car and began to talk to me like I was a long lost friend. She asked if I knew of any available apartments in the area (I didn't), if I liked camping in the nude (I said something about bugs), and whether I'd be interested in taking a drive in her car to get some ice cream (well, sure). Before I knew what hit me, I was in this woman's car and we were pulling onto the highway. Probably not a good idea . . . but still, it was a hot day and who doesn't love ice cream?

She said she had to find a new place to live because her neighbors were starting to complain about the noise coming from her apartment. "What kind of noise?" I asked, fervently hoping that the word "chainsaw" would not figure prominently in her response. "Sex noise," she said, her eyes fixed on the road. "When I come, it's like an earthquake." That's what she said. I had known this woman for maybe twenty minutes. I started to look around the car for the handcuffs and rope.

We spent the rest of the day driving around aimlessly, trad-
ing variations of our life stories. She said she was a fashion
model. I told her that I liked to write poetry. Later, as she
was dropping me back off at my car, she asked if I wanted
to come by her apartment that night. She wanted to "check
out" my writing. Just as I was thinking that it might not be
such a good idea, my thoughts inexplicably turned to the
San Andreas fault. I jotted down the directions.

I was trembling with anticipation as I climbed the stairs to her apartment. To my delight she answered the door dressed in a blue nightgown. She invited me in and told me to make myself comfortable on the couch. "Do you like jazz?" she asked. She moved over to the stereo and placed what appeared to be her only album on the turntable. Seconds later, the theme from *Peter Gunn* by Henry Mancini was filling the room at a volume capable of cracking plaster. I was clearly doomed.

89

When the song stopped, she ran into the bedroom and returned with a photo album. It was her modeling portfolio. She sat down next to me on the couch and began flipping through the pages. The first few photos were fairly innocuous; basic head shots, assorted shoots for trade magazines (her in hot pants straddling a lawn tractor). Then came the "artistic" nudes; satin sheets, spurs, cowboy boots, etc. After a few pages of escalating wonderment, she offered to give me a massage.

I stripped to my underwear and she proceeded to rub oil all over my exposed acreage. After about forty seconds, I suggested that she should take off her nightgown so I could apply some therapy in her direction. With that, she got up and disappeared into the bedroom. I unstuck myself from the couch and started to follow. Before I got too far, she was back, wrapped in a bathrobe. "It's getting late, thanks for stopping by." I stood there, perplexed, glistening and spectacularly unfulfilled.

Summer was over. It was time to put failed seduction at-
tempts and crappy security jobs behind me. College was
kicking into gear again and it was a welcome intervention.
Now that I was back in Boston and surrounded by my fellow seekers of higher education, I could focus on more
refined pursuits — like dorm room bong-a-thons and par-
ties featuring garbage cans filled with fruit punch and grain
alcohol. In other words, the life of the mind.

When I wasn't tampering with my brain chemistry, I was preparing for a career in radio broadcasting. I was intrigued by the creative possibilities of the medium. Not to mention the pay-ola, drug-ola, and general all-around "ola." Alas, by the time I was released from the broadcasting trout farm, the disco virus had all but destroyed free-form radio. The industry was being held hostage by morons in satin baseball jackets with tiny coke spoons around their necks.

The closest I came to a radio gig was a graduation-mandated internship at a radio station in my hometown. The station was a low-watt operation whose primary audience consisted of senior citizens and other listeners with limited ability to change the dial. The programming was evenly divided between oldies and hemorrhoid ointment testimonials. As an intern, I was relegated to making coffee, ripping copy off the AP wire, and getting in the way of people trying to make a living.

One of my favorite meaningless tasks was recording the daily message for the station's "weather line" — a community service designed for any poor soul who had access to a phone but was unable to look out the window to see if it was raining. Each day they'd give me the weather report to read and leave me alone with the answering machine. It wasn't long before "increasing locusts" and "steady rain of toads" started showing up in the forecast. Better bring an umbrella!

Every once in a while they'd release me into the wild to conduct "man on the street" interviews. The idea was that I'd poll the public on a topic of local interest ("Are you in favor of the proposed sewage treatment theme park?") and then go back to the station and edit the responses into a shiny chunk of processed info-tainment. A great theory. But the reality was that the only people who were willing to participate in my silly surveys were certifiably insane.

If I was serious about a career in radio, I would have tried to finagle a full-time gig when my internship ended. But my heart just wasn't in it. In the radio biz, you were expected to start out at a small station in a small market (Good Morning, Toledo!) and then grind your way up the ladder, until you finally landed a rockin' "drive time" shift in a major city. This slow dues-paying initiation process explains why the hip DJ in town is usually a cranky guy in his fifties with a bad toupee.

I didn't want to pay dues. I wanted artistic control! So I left radio behind and took a job vacuuming carpets at an apartment complex. I vacuumed every inch — the halls, the stairs — everywhere and every day. When I shut my eyes, I can still see the maroon-colored chain link pattern. The only thing that kept me going was my fantasy that one day a sexually frustrated housewife would appear in an apartment doorway and beg me to apply suction to her sectional living room set.

One morning while a coworker and I were loitering in a stairwell, a frantic young woman appeared in the hall and asked if we knew CPR. We followed her into her apartment and she pointed to her unconscious friend on the couch. She had swallowed too many pills of too many types in too short a time. My friend performed the mouth-to-mouth maneuver while I assisted by pacing back and forth. Within moments the ambulance arrived and we went back to vacuuming.

I wandered around the rest of the day bumping into walls and dropping hose attachments down the stairs. Here was the most innocuous form of employment in the universe and reality still managed to find me. Vacuuming and tending to overdose victims was not a good mix. At the end of my shift, I turned in my equipment and collected my final check. To be honest, I can't even recall how I got the damn job or where the apartment complex was located. I think I had the job for ten days.

4

ROCK STAR PETTING ZOO

Since I was now officially "between opportunities," I turned to the one thing I could always count on — music. There was a new record store in town called Raspberries, so I decided to give them whatever was left in my wallet. I had picked up the new Jonathan Richman album and was heading out the door when I noticed a "Help Wanted" sign. I went back in and talked to the store's manager, an aging Paul McCartney wanna-be named Paul Ray. He said he'd call me the next day.

I didn't hold out much hope that I would get the job. Working at a record store was (and probably still is) one of the most desirable forms of slave labor. The idea that you could get paid to listen to music and make snide comments about bands you didn't like was too good to be true. So I was thrilled when Paul called to tell me the job was mine. The way I looked at it, someone was going to pay me to do something that I'd be doing anyway. I had definitely turned a corner.

The job consisted of sorting, pricing and shelving albums. After a few weeks of slapping stickers on every slab of vinyl that came through the door, I managed to commit to memory a truly insufferable quantity of music trivia. I could pick up any album and tell you when it was released, how it stood critically in comparison with the band's past efforts, when the bass player OD'd, pretty much everything. Just what the world needed — one more record store snob.

The record-buying public would dutifully line up for whatever new flavor of dog food they were playing on the radio. It was the lowest common denominator principle of mass consumerism. Pavlov's big salivating jukebox. One example of this reflex in action was the *Saturday Night Fever* soundtrack. The sales of this sonic abomination were astronomical. Semis were pulling up to the store every ten minutes to deliver more of the coveted disco poop.

Record companies paid a fee to have albums played in the store and MCA was paying big bucks to push *Saturday Night Fever*. The more they paid, the more we played. During the course of one cruel month we were forced to listen to the thing in its excruciating entirety at least three times a day. It was torture by falsetto. It made us all cranky as hell, compounded by the fact that everyone who came into the store loved the album. Stayin' alive, stayin' alive, etc.

The best thing about being a record store snob was the endless supply of records, concert tickets and other wampum doled out by the record company weasels. The free stuff was given to the manager, who trickled the trinkets down to the clerks. If you laughed at his jokes, you might get the new Blondie album. If you got him a date with one of the teenage cashiers, you could wind up backstage with Tom Petty's guitar tech, sipping complimentary cocktails.

Another Raspberries staple was the "Midnight Sale," wherein crowds would line up late at night for the privilege of purchasing barely-discounted merchandise. Before one such sale, a record company rep came by and handed out Devo suits for us all to wear. So we did. But not before sneaking out back to ingest non-traditional intoxicants. At midnight they opened the doors and there I was, fully de-evolved, surrounded crazed shoppers waving disco albums.

The main Raspberries store in Boston routinely hosted promotional appearances by lower-tier rock stars. These heavily promoted pony shows, known as "in-stores," were nothing more than an elaborate form of record company lubricant designed to shift more units. The artists (ahem) begrudgingly put up with the indignity of meeting the public as a way to please the record company, and in doing so hopefully forestall their inevitable future careers as used car salesmen.

In-stores were a big hit with the fans, but if you were stuck working the event, it was pretty much just another day at the office. Except in the corner of the office there was a pouting artiste signing autographs. It was like hosting a rock star petting zoo. But we didn't know that at the time. All we knew was that the Boston store was getting all the action and we wanted some. So we begged Paul to arrange an in-store appearance we could call our own.

After numerous complaints about our store not getting any respect, the big day finally arrived. Paul called us together for the announcement. "I'm happy to report that the guys at headquarters finally listened. We've got a in-store scheduled for next weekend." Who could it be? Cheap Trick? Elvis Costello? Paul paused a beat, looked down at the floor and said, "It's The Village People." It was the quintessential "be careful what you wish for" moment.

On the fateful day we dutifully festooned the store with all manner of Village People propaganda until it resembled a veritable Fire Island carnival ride. The crowd that showed up to see "the band" consisted almost exclusively of small gay men and their queen-sized female friends. We all waited. We waited some more. Eventually, a limo pulled up and in walked our guests of honor in full costumed regalia, trailed by a phalanx of record company life forms.

I wish I could say the guys were down-to-earth and not just stereotypes in Halloween costumes. No such luck. From the moment they arrived, until the limo carted them away, they did nothing but whine. They complained about the coffee, they complained about the crowd. They even bitched about the pens we provided for autographs. I actually had to go out and buy new pens. I asked the cashier, "Do these look like pens The Village People might enjoy?"

It wasn't always that exciting. In fact, most of the time it was excruciatingly tedious. I endured the long winter days by straightening the Iggy Pop bin and folding and refolding Kiss t-shirts. On one occasion, when the cabin fever was particularly unbearable, I filled out entry forms for a contest that the store was sponsoring with a local radio station. The grand prize was an all-expenses paid trip to Jamaica. Employees were ineligible, but I was bored. I filled out about a hundred entries.

A week later, my friend Mark called the store to tell me that he'd heard my name on the radio. My name had been drawn as the winner of the contest. All I had to do was call the station to claim my prize. I dialed the number. Another friend, who worked at the station, answered the phone. He asked if I still worked at Raspberries. It was a moral dilemma. Was a free trip to a tropical resort worth lying to a friend? I paused a second. "I do not!" I replied.

It seemed only right to offer the other ticket to Mark. We couldn't believe our luck — we were going to escape the New England winter and party like Bob Marley! On the day before our trip, a blizzard dumped three feet of snow on the Northeast. Our bags were packed when the governor came on TV in an elaborate sweater and declared a state of emergency. After three days of slurred negotiations with Air Jamaica we were airlifted out of Massachusetts.

Between the airport and the bumpy cab ride to the hotel, Mark managed to trade all of his cigarettes for cartoon-size spliffs. It seemed like a good deal at the time. It wasn't until we got to the hotel that we learned that there hadn't been any cigarettes on the island for two months. Luckily, I had quit smoking a year before the trip. Mark was not so lucky. He spent the rest of the week inhaling cigars and coughing up what appeared to be chunks of molten lava.

Most of the tourist information we encountered suggested that we should stick close to the hotel after dark and not wander into the hills in search of adventure. We took this advice with a few grains of salt and several festive rum drinks. Surely this type of advice was designed to protect the less streetwise tourist and did not apply to us. We decided to forgo the hotel-sponsored limbo contest and go wandering into the hills. This is what rum will do to you.

Our plan was to try to find the bar that our new friend, the ever-cheerful hotel bartender, had recommended. After staggering for a mile or so in the dark, down a street that was nothing more than a dirt path, we came upon what appeared to be our destination — a dilapidated shack that looked like it was made out of scraps of corrugated metal. Above the door was a blinking sign that read "Go-Go Bar." This did not look to be a regular tourist destination.

The inside of the bar was nothing too elaborate — just a few picnic tables and a bar along one side. The bartender, a huge individual without a shirt, was doubling as the club DJ. When we came in he was dragging the needle off one reggae album and slapping it down on another slice. When the music started, women in mini skirts jumped up on the picnic tables and began to "go-go dance"; a half-hearted pelvic movement with leftover 60s-era embellishment.

We made our way over to the bartender and traded bright-ly-colored currency for two local beers. In no time we were beset by go-go dancers of every conceivable permutation. There were at least fifteen dancers vying for our attention, each of them telling us how much they loved us, each of them trying to remove money from our wallets. The experience quickly went from hilarious to terrifying. Somehow we managed to escape their clutches and survive the rest of the trip.

There was a surprise waiting for me when I returned to Raspberries. After a year of enjoying the carefree existence of a clerk, someone had arrived at the idea that I should be promoted to assistant manager. How could this be? I had demonstrated zero initiative. I showed up late for work and checked out early. Yet somehow that couldn't-care-less attitude translated into management potential. My minimum wage honeymoon was drawing to a close.

I could have worked there forever, straightening the bins and dispensing advice ("back away from the Ace Frehley solo album!"), but being assistant manager was a drag. The worst part was reconciling the register at the end of the night. If the total was over, we'd just keep the extra money. But if the amount was under, I'd be trapped for hours with the cashier du jour reliving every transaction until we tracked down the missing money. Have I mentioned I'm not very good at math?

I started to take out my frustration on the store playlist. After three weeks of listening to the latest Barry Manilow tour de force, I could feel my brain beginning to melt. So I decided to use my new assistant manager powers for evil, not good. If I didn't like an album, I would play it, but at the wrong speed. (Sales of an Alvin Lee album actually increased when we played it a 45 rpm.) At closing time, I'd put on Captain Beefheart and other surefire crowd-pleasers to clear the store.

When I look back on this, it's clear that all this mucking around with the rules was just a subconscious cry for help. I didn't know it at the time, but I was looking to get fired. I was much more comfortable being in a position where I could question authority. Now that I was stuck between being an hourly-wage drone and management, the battle lines were blurred and the end was near. My tray table was in the upright locked position. I was going down fast.

The catalyst of my undoing was the new dress code. Somehow, for some reason, the powers-that-be decided it would be fun to make everyone wear red vests with a big embroidered raspberry on the back. I couldn't believe it! Memories of cowboy uniforms and security badges came flooding back. I'd sworn that I'd never wear another uniform, and now I was supposed to enforce this idiocy. Something deep inside my head made a popping sound.

The grand finale went something like this: It was an hour before closing time and I was taking a turn at the register. The Grateful Dead's *Europe '72* album (not on the playlist, needless to say) was blasting over the store sound system. We had arrived at the part of the Dead's set where Jerry and the boys are in full feedback mode. It was my favorite part. But to the uninitiated, it probably sounded like a polka band being forced sideways through a screen door.

At the precise moment that Jerry's pharmaceutically-aid-ed enlightenment reached its apex, Paul Ray walked into the store with a sinister-looking stranger. He walked up to me and introduced his companion. It was the new district manager. Whoops. Paul cocked his head slightly, glancing up at the overhead speaker, the blood slowly draining from his face. "What's that?" he stammered. My mind raced through that week's playlist titles. "It's the new Peter Frampton album," I said.

The three of us stood there in silence. I made the Peter Frampton comment. It was up to Paul to return volley. As I waited, I glanced over Paul's shoulder to the back of the store. There, emerging from the back room, were the clerks and cashiers, trailed by a THC-enriched fog. Even worse, they were not wearing the requisite red vests. It was the unholy trinity of Jerry Garcia, illegal substance abuse and fashion insubordination that proved to be my undoing.

The next morning when I showed up for work, Paul said that someone from the main office was waiting to see me in the back room. No surprise, really. I knew what was coming. It was time to be sized for the cement kimono. The meeting was short and painless. The enforcer, I think his name was Vinny, asked me to sign a form, effectively terminating my employment. It didn't seem wise to argue. I had been there for a year and a half — a personal record.

I made the rounds of the other record stores in town that day, figuring that my wealth of experience would be a valuable asset to the competition. The interviews all went well until they asked me why I left Raspberries. I either lied ("I need a new challenge!") or threw myself on the mercy of the court ("I was framed!"). Both approaches failed. I was damaged goods. There was nothing left to do but watch *Celebrity Billiards* and scan the help wanted ads.

A few days later, I spotted a promising ad: "Material Handler, $5.00 per Hour." This was back in the day when five bucks was the fiscal dividing line between basic grunt work and prestigious grunt work. I called the number and spoke to a woman who was running a temp agency. She asked if I'd have any trouble lifting heavy objects and working with older women. I paused to imagine various scenarios involving those two elements. "Uh, no," I heard myself say.

5

COUNT YOUR REVOLUTIONS

I was told to report to Digitrex Corporation, a huge computer company that at the time seemed to employ just about half of everyone in Massachusetts. I jotted down the name and number of my new boss (Bill) and hung up the phone. I was excited to hear that I'd be working at a real company like Digitrex. It was time to say goodbye to washing dishes, suctioning carpet fiber and fetching pens for mediocre celebrities. I was about to join the exciting and professional world of high tech.

That night I dreamed that I was working in a futuristic office park. It was a real Stanley Kubrick carnival ride, complete with moving sidewalks and guys in lab coats. The real Digitrex turned out to be nothing like my sci-fi dream. It was just a nondescript metal box warehouse in the middle of a nondescript suburban setting. When I arrived, I called the number the temp agency gave me and waited in the lobby. A few minutes later, Bill showed up and offered to give me a tour.

Bill led me into the belly of the warehouse beast. It wasn't long before I began to grasp the gravity of my new employment opportunity. The first thing that hit me was the heat. It was easily over one hundred degrees inside the warehouse. The second thing that nearly hit me was one of the dazed-looking forklift operators who were hurtling back and forth in every direction. They were all laughing, yelling obscenities at each other. Bill just shrugged and said, "It's after lunch."

We arrived at a clearing where women dressed in blue smocks were shuffling around tables stacked with software manuals. They were placing the manuals into cardboard boxes and then placing the boxes on the floor. It was a strange sight, compounded by the physical properties of the women themselves. They were all short, all in their mid-fifties and all puffing cigarettes. My high tech job was to assist these Smurfs by stacking the filled boxes onto pallets.

Bill waved goodbye and left me alone to fend for myself. So I started stacking boxes. After I topped off the first pallet, one of the Smurfs yelled to a passing forklift operator, who skidded to a halt and removed the finished product. So I stacked another. And so on. After about five minutes of this, my thoughts started to drift. While my physical half was still tethered to the warehouse, my mind was on vacation, applying suntan lotion to a giggling island girl somewhere on the coast of Tahiti.

Eventually, the gals took a break and filed off to the cafeteria. (I recall them walking off in a line, whistling a tune, but I may be confusing that memory with *Sleeping Beauty*.) Now that I had fifteen minutes to kill, I decided to take a tour of the warehouse and try to get the lay of the land. There appeared to be three distinct enclaves: production, shipping, and receiving. As I moved from one area to the other, I half-expected to be stopped by the border patrol.

Taking orders from the Smurfs put me at the bottom of the warehouse pecking order, but I didn't see any means of escape. Then I met Jimbo, one of the shippers whose job it was to pick up the full pallets. At least the shippers appeared to be having fun, and Jimbo seemed to be having the most fun of all. One afternoon, as he was stopping by to pick up a pallet, he caught my eye and silently-mouthed the words that came to define my early days at Digitrex — "Wanna get high?"

It was just about break time, so I decided to take Jimbo up on his offer. We had three breaks each day: fifteen minutes in the morning, thirty minutes at midday for lunch, followed by fifteen minutes in the afternoon. The Smurfs dutifully took their breaks in the cafeteria. Everyone else ran out of the building, jumped into their cars and roared out of the parking lot, hell-bent on consumption (beer, weed, aerosol cheese, whadda ya got?). Jimbo was the break Zen Master.

After I had spent about a week on the box-packing chain gang, Jimbo used his influence with management to get me a gig helping him in the consolidation area — the corner of the warehouse where all of the outgoing orders (boxes, boxes and more boxes) were sent to be prepared for shipping. The area consisted of two beat-up desks surrounded by a ten-foot chain link fence. Across from the desks, protruding through the fence, was the tail end of a conveyer belt. My new office was a cage.

I didn't mind working in a cage — mostly because I had a desk to call my own. Sure, it was rusting in spots, the drawers didn't work and one leg was shorter than the others, but it was all mine. And as I sat there, sipping my industrial coffee/sludge and gazing out at the warehouse through the holes in the cage, I felt at peace with the world. Then the conveyer started. Jimbo choked down the last of his coffee and handed me a clipboard. "Here we go," he said.

It turned out that we were responsible for "consolidating" every box packed in the warehouse. Each box had a unique number and every number corresponded to one of approximately five million different destination points. Our job was to find the number on the boxes as they came shooting down the conveyer belt and then deposit each box on the correct pallet. It was a simple process when the flow was slow and steady. When it was busy, it was a bad *I Love Lucy* episode.

When the box parade reached warp speed any distraction could spell trouble. If you couldn't keep up, boxes would start shooting off the conveyer onto the floor. The only way to stop the onslaught was to wedge a broomstick into the works. This was effective, but not without its own consequences. The belt, now dangerously overloaded, would start to sway back and forth, forcing boxes over the side and onto the heads of unsuspecting bystanders.

After a month of witnessing my superior box-sorting skills, Bill offered me a full-time job at $4.90 an hour, a dime below my temp wage. I almost turned it down. After all, there was my imaginary career in radio broadcasting to consider. In the end, I couldn't resist all the benefits that went along with a job at Digitrex. It was a veritable security blanket of pensions, paid vacations, life insurance and healthcare coverage. But the real clincher was the free shoes.

That's right, free shoes were part of the deal. And sure enough, a week later, the "shoe truck" pulled up to the warehouse. It was sort of a letdown. Instead of rows of stylish footwear, there was just a burly guy sitting in front of a hundred pairs of the same shoe, a Frankenstein-style work boot with a steel toe. They were ugly, uncomfortable and weighed about ten pounds each. Instead of providing protection from the fork trucks, they just made it more difficult to run away.

I was no longer just a rented slab of beef. I was part of the Digitrex family. Since I was going to be there for a while, it was time to get serious and try to make sense of my surroundings. It wasn't easy. Everyone operated in constant overdrive, passing paperwork and boxes to each other like they were trying to win some sort of blue-collar relay race. I decided to try to get some answers from Louie, one of the seasoned (pickled) Digitrex veterans. Eventually, I cracked the code.

The warehouse was like any other food chain. Identifying the subtle shading of dominance amongst the various job functions was the key to survival. According to my field studies, the bottom of the chain was occupied by the pickers. Using only a shopping list, a metal cart and whatever malt liquor was still in their bloodstream from the night before, the pickers spent their days locating, counting and "picking" the pieces and parts that made up each order.

Pickers tended to be ex-carnival workers, aspiring convicts and local girls with lots of purple eyeliner. My favorite picker was Ed, a befuddled gentleman who was famous for urinating into the water cooler basins. I'll never forget the day a group of Asian dignitaries took a tour of the warehouse. As the tour was passing by, Ed emerged from the men's room with his by then ubiquitous male protuberance on full patriotic display. We could not have been more proud.

Then there were the packers. This female-dominated gang was in charge of collating and packing the manuals and magnetic media supplied by the pickers. This highly repetitive function was ideally suited for individuals with sharp motor skills and an eye for detail. But that was hard to come by. So instead they settled for chain-smoking hard-drinkin' women in their late fifties with silver hair. They had names like Dot and Rose. They meant business.

Holding it all together was my group, the material handlers. Our lot in life was miscellaneous hauling and helping, and "other duties as required." Mostly we hung out with the shippers and receivers. The receivers unloaded the incoming trucks and stocked the warehouse with the raw materials that were later picked by pickers and packed by packers. The shippers loaded the finished finery onto waiting trucks. Trucks pulled in. Trucks pulled out. Lather, rinse and repeat.

Wedged into the middle of this madness were the office drones; supervisors and miscellaneous middle management types responsible for riding herd over the aforementioned unwashed. I'd venture to say that most of them didn't have the requisite gray matter to run a frozen yogurt franchise, let alone a software distribution network. The absolute cream of this failed crop was a distinctly unpleasant authority figure named Edna. More on her later.

Eventually Jimbo moved over to the shipping department, leaving me in control of the consolidation area. I liked working with Jimbo, but I saw his move as an opportunity to advance my own personal aesthetic. Now that I was running the joint, I set about transforming the area into a hipster oasis. I put up posters and other found art on the walls and turned up the radio. I was determined to make it the coolest cage in a dark corner of a warehouse, ever.

Other lost souls began frequenting the cage; notables such as Jeff and Phil, a pair of box-schleppers who shared my appetite for fringe music and left-of-center fun. Leo was another prominent player in this working class saga. He started off as a temporary janitor, but graduated to the loftier material handler title in no time. We knew Leo was destined to join our gang when we discovered him sleeping on a rock out on the front lawn of the warehouse.

Another one of my early Digitrex co-conspirators was a second shift supervisor named Al. When he first got the job, I noticed that he spent most of his dinner breaks sitting outside in his car. I thought he was a loner. It turned out he just liked to spend his quality time with a tiny blue hash pipe. Whenever I worked late and our shifts overlapped, we'd drive around at break time listening to a nightly children's story hour on the radio. It must have made for an odd sight.

Rounding out the cast were supporting players — characters like Frank, the befuddled packer who one day decided to hitchhike to Florida, leaving behind all of his personal belongings; Carl, the beyond-flamboyant office worker who was arrested at a highway rest area for playing pinochle with a fallen member of the clergy; and Ricardo, the chain-smoking Latino coordinator who proudly cheated on his wife with the one-eyed picker known as Sweet Helga.

A daily regimen of restorative naps and bootleg pharmaceutical consumption made life on the high tech chain gang nearly tolerable. Yes, everything was along the lines of fine until the god of futile labor presented us with a new metaphorical ditch to dig. Our mettle was tested. Our cages rattled. Our brains removed and replaced slightly askew. The force of nature capable of this biblical-quality upheaval was the aforementioned Edna, our new supervisor.

After months of doing whatever we wanted, we were ill-prepared for the unrelenting scrutiny and micromanagement that were the linchpins of Edna's supervisory style. She was an evil presence in sensible shoes, metering out "warnings" (verbal and written) to any fool who questioned her wisdom. At least once a week I'd find myself in her office, pleading my case over one infraction or another. The only things missing were thigh-high patent leather boots and a riding crop.

One summer afternoon, when the temperature topped one hundred degrees, we decided to go swimming at lunch. We had only thirty minutes to accomplish this prison break (we were supposed to eat in the cafe, where the loaf du jour was spiced with saltpeter and lithium), so we had to be quick. Factoring in departure and arrival coordinates, we figured that we had precisely nineteen minutes to get wet and get back. It was a perfect plan. Then we forgot to bring a watch.

Edna was waiting for us when we returned. By her calcu-
lation, we were an inexcusable five minutes late. I coun-
tered that there was no "real time" because the warehouse
clocks were all different. An imaginative but unsuccessful
defense. Our heads were destined for Edna's trophy room.
We were promptly placed on "probation" (one more strike
and you're fired) and the clocks were synchronized. From
that point on Edna tracked our every movement.

Being on probation didn't change my day-to-day existence, which mostly consisted of stacking boxes on pallets and then securing said boxes to said pallet so the unit could be hauled away. We had been using metal strapping to keep the boxes in place, but the new technology in town was shrink-wrap. Instead of dealing with sharp metal straps, you just walked in circles around the pallet until the sucker was sufficiently mummified. We also tried it on desks, cars and each other.

Using the shrink-wrap was a vast improvement over the hard-to-handle metal (I still have scars from being whapped by errant straps). But there was something about us being so happy that triggered Edna's internal alarm. One morning, before I had my first sip of coffee, she materialized next to my desk (imagine a B-movie vampire) and said she was concerned that the wrap was too expensive. She wanted to study the "relative cost differential." I braced myself.

Swiped from Xaime

This exact conversation followed: Edna: "How many times do you walk around each skid?" Me: "Huh?" Edna: "I need to know your revolutions." Me: "My what?" Edna: "How many times you walk around each skid to shrink-wrap it." Me: "What?" Edna: "I want you to count your revolutions and keep track of the totals!" She handed me a stack of freshly-concocted forms for noting my "revolutions." I looked at the forms. I looked at Edna. I looked at the forms. I looked at Edna. Me: "Fuck you."

We stood staring at each other. Neither one of us was quite sure what was supposed to happen next. I had just told her to fuck off. I couldn't think of anything to add — it seemed like a complete thought. Eventually, she spoke. "That was not necessary, Mr. Beaupre." She threw the forms on my desk. "Make sure you keep an accurate count!" She spun with military precision on the heels of her steel-toe executive pumps and marched off. It was a close call indeed.

I have no idea why she didn't summon the security goons and have them toss me out the front door. I could only conclude that while she had every intention of firing me, the timing wasn't right. I'd be damned if I was going to wait around while she looked for the perfect apple to stuff into my impertinent mouth. I decided to interview for a position in the receiving department. I didn't want to leave Digitrex. I just had to leave the Edna-controlled zone.

Transferring to a new job was a perfect way to escape Edna's clutches while garnering a modest raise at the same time. But I almost didn't get the job. Walter, the low-key manager in charge of the receiver gang, had heard rumors about my "attitude." Edna was poisoning the well, telling everyone that I was a "hippie" who couldn't be trusted. I assured Walter that I wouldn't burn any flags or spike the water cooler with LSD. He hired me, god bless him.

Instead of managing my own corner of the warehouse, I was now part of a team. Our job was to unload the incoming trucks, verify the contents and then enter assorted information into the receiving system (my first encounter with a computer). We were a jolly bunch, with the exception of Quiet Jim, a brooding Viet Nam vet, and Big Doris, an aging female wrestler in a "Happy Days" school sweater. Doris didn't like me. She expressed this by breaking my coffee mugs.

Things were fine until Walter was replaced by Fred, a head case with "biting issues." Whenever he got angry (at least three times a shift), he would start gnawing like a rabid schnauzer on the nearest box of manuals. His reign of terror was short-lived. A month later, management announced that the operation was moving to a new building an hour away. The bad news was that the new facility already had its own receiving squad. I had thirty days to find a job.

169

6

BRUNO'S LEFT HAND

With only a month to secure a new unskilled career, time was of the essence. Every morning when I got to work, I'd check the list of jobs moving to the new warehouse to see if there were any openings. Eventually I spotted a listing for a second shift computer operator. I had zero compu- ter skills, but they were "willing to train." I called the hir- ing manager, who seemed oddly thrilled to hear from me. He asked me to come in for an interview the next day.

When I arrived for my interview, I was struck by how different the computer room was from the warehouse. Instead of the frenzy of the production floor, I found myself in a chilly, brightly lit space filled with rows of humming hardware. I stopped at one of the computers and leaned in for a closer look. "Hello, Steve," it said. I stared like a perplexed farm animal at the talking technology until a short bald man emerged from behind the machine. It was Joe, the group's manager.

The interview lasted five minutes. Joe didn't care about my warehouse job. Instead, he talked up the advantages of the four-day workweek and casually mentioned that if I "joined the team" I would have to work in the computer room for at least one year before I could transfer to another Digitrex job. When I asked about the job itself, he said, "Don't worry, we will train you." These are warning signs. I ignored them all and shook his hand. "Welcome aboard," he said.

After I signed on the dotted line, Joe took me on a tour of the computer room. I now noticed that there were actual human beings seated between the rows of hardware. These were my fellow "operators." No one looked up as we passed by. Instead they just stared into space, their eyes fixed somewhere off in the distance, while their hands were busy labeling and stacking computer tapes. I tried to imagine myself seated next to one of these undead automatons. It was easier than I would have liked.

The tour of the computer room left me utterly disillusioned. This was not the type of job I had envisioned. I had imagined myself wearing a lab coat, wandering from computer to computer making cryptic notations on a clipboard. After a long day at the office, I would retire to my hipster bachelor hideaway, where I would drink top-shelf scotch from a thick glass tumbler, listen to Miles Davis' *Kind of Blue*, and brood endlessly about "the work." OK, I was a bit naïve.

175

Being a computer operator was about as exciting as being a toaster oven operator. The job required zero brain activity. Strapping boxes to skids was quantum physics compared to this gig. When you stripped away all the futuristic props and jargon, it was just a glorified assembly line. But instead of manufacturing inflatable athletic shoes or some other coveted consumer item, my job was to encode and label floppy discs and rolls of magnetic computer tape.

Joe showed me which buttons to push and when. It was like one of those documentaries where scientists teach a porpoise to spell its name using fish treat reinforcement. Only I was *not* getting any fish treats. The drill went like this: Take a blank tape. Strap it to the machine. Press the start button. When the tape stops spinning (anywhere from ten seconds to thirty minutes later), slap a label on it and stack it in a plastic bin. Repeat three hundred times.

After learning the intricacies of tape production, I graduated to the second shift, four-day workweek schedule. The prospect of long weekends and sleeping late sounded appealing. Wrong again. To earn the extra day of freedom, a pound of flesh was extracted in the form of four straight ten-hour days. Throw in a little overtime and you could easily be looking at a hellish twelve-hour endurance session. Ankle chains and bowls of gruel sold separately.

It wasn't long before the new schedule wreaked havoc on my social life. I felt as if I'd been exiled to a parallel universe apart from all my friends. My free time, what there was left of it, took place when no one else was around. At night, driving home from work, it was just me and the truckers hauling produce. During the day, when I'd go out to do an errand, I was surrounded by hordes of slow-moving octogenarians. To compensate for the isolation, I began to work longer shifts.

One night Joe asked for volunteers to stay late and make floppy disk labels. I signed on, along with Gary, one of the other operators. We were shocked that no one else volunteered. That is until Joe introduced us to the Brunheiser Label King (known to the villagers as "Evil Bruno"). It was a nasty contraption that resembled a cross between a drill press and a 17th century torture device. We listened intently as Joe explained the care and feeding of our new mechanical friend.

Before we could think about doing any printing, we had to set the type to be printed on the labels. This was accomplished (in theory) by inserting and lining up (just right) a series of tiny rubber stamps, each containing one number, onto a metal plate. The metal plate would then be clamped to a hammer-type device ("Bruno's left hand"), which, when activated, would slam down on the blank label as it passed by on the conveyer belt. What could go wrong?

An hour of pure frustration later, we had twelve labels and there were still five hundred left to do. Clearly we needed to focus. So we went out to my car and drank whiskey. It was the coldest night of the year (three below zero), but we needed to put some distance between ourselves and Bruno. When we got back, things fell into place and a new plan emerged: Gary would work the start button, while I plunged my hands into the machine to guide the labels.

Our strategy worked flawlessly up until the point when I yelled "Stop!" and Gary heard it as "Now!" Instead of pressing the red button, he pressed the green button. A simple mistake, really. Before I could retract my hand, Bruno's left hand slammed down on my thumb, leaving behind a perfectly printed part number and a two-inch blood-spurting gash. We stood looking at each other. I was wavering on my feet. Gary was laughing. I staggered off to the bathroom to inspect my thumb.

I wrapped my thumb with paper towels and secured the throbbing mess with electrical tape. This seemed like a good time to leave, so I waved goodbye to Gary and staggered out to my car. A mile down the road, the car sputtered to a stop. I was out of gas. Perfect. I abandoned the car and began walking. There I was, on a deserted road at four in the morning on the coldest night in living memory, hitching a ride with an injured thumb. Jean Paul Sartre, white courtesy telephone.

Just as I was about to freeze in place by the side of the road, headlights appeared on the horizon. The oncoming car was weaving all over the road. I was either going to be rescued or run over. Luckily, the driver timed his approach perfectly and skidded into a snow bank just a few feet away. My Good Samaritan was blind drunk, but I didn't care. I pushed his car out of the snow and he returned the favor by giving me a ride home. We hit four more snow banks before we got to my apartment.

A week before we were supposed to move to the new warehouse, Joe arranged for us to take a tour of the building's computer room. The plan was that we would drive to the new warehouse, take the tour with Joe and then rush back to the old building for our regular shift. Road trip! On the afternoon of the tour we packed a few coolers with beer and began a processional to our new home. By the time we got there we had a suitable radioactive glow.

When the tour was over we told Joe we'd see him back at the computer room. Instead, we decided to check out the town's nightlife. All we could find was a seedy VFW bar. We pledged to have one beer and return to work. Six pitchers later a better idea surfaced. We'd all call in sick. One by one, we called Joe on the bar pay phone, each of us making up our own sorry excuse. Unfortunately, the same jukebox song was playing in the background for each call.

The next afternoon Joe called us into his office. He still looked angry. He clearly wanted to fire us, but he really couldn't. No one else was crazy enough to take these jobs. So he put us all on six-month probation, effectively extending our one-year commitments to eighteen months. At this rate, I'd never get out! Something had to change. If I was ever going to climb the corporate ladder, I'd need to make better decisions. Lab rats could figure this stuff out. Surely, I could.

Having a job in the computer room was like trying to work off a prison sentence. Sure, it was fun to spend your days harassing the guards in the exercise yard. But bad behavior was best left to the lifers with no possibility for parole. A smart inmate had a better plan. If you wanted to leave, you had to pretend you wanted to stay. I was determined not to live out my days chained to a tape machine. I would dig my personal escape tunnel by pretending to be a model prisoner.

From that point on, I was a changed man. I volunteered to train new employees. I helped to schedule the nightly tape production. I even asked Joe to put me on an accelerated training regimen so that I could earn a promotion. The ugliness of the first six months was a distant memory. I was Joe's golden boy. Now that I was rehabilitated, I had to get out before the happy dust wore off. I put the word out on the street that I needed to be sprung, and fast.

I'd put in just over a year of hard time when I received some good news. Al and Leo from the original warehouse gang had landed shipper/receiver jobs at two neighboring Digitrex office buildings. These were dream gigs, combining blue-collar autocracy with a no-heavy-lifting white-collar ambiance. And the best part was that they had convinced their boss to hire a third person to help out between the two buildings. This was my ticket out of tape hell.

In the computer room, misery not only loved company, it demanded it contractually. If I was going to make a break, my exit strategy had to be perfect. I figured that if I timed everything just right, the new job offer would coincide with the conclusion of my eighteen-month sentence and I'd be a free man. Fortunately, my second shift schedule allowed ample opportunity to arrange a clandestine interview with my boss-man-to-be, a mysterious figure known as The Wooden Man.

I showed up for the interview with a snazzy conserva-
tive haircut. Not that it was necessary. The Wooden Man
was just an old fart in golf slacks who cared more about
recounting the highlights of his storied career than asking
about my meager qualifications. After an hour of blathering
about his accomplishments, he concluded by saying how
great it would be to have "the three best shipper/receivers
in all of Digitrex" on his team. Al and Leo clearly had this
poor guy snowed.

There was just one more hurdle before I could accept the job. Since I was still three weeks shy of completing my computer room sentence, I had to convince Joe to sign my exit papers. When I showed up for work with my release form tucked into a folder, Joe asked to see me. What was this, some sort of preemptive strike!? I took a seat across from him in his office. He had a weird grin on his face. He was clutching a folder just like mine. We were like a couple of gunslingers.

Throwing caution to the wind, I drew first and confessed my infidelity. It was true — I had been sneaking off to meet with another manager and I had been offered a new job! Joe was shocked. He opened his folder and passed its contents across the table. It was an official letter, congratulating me on my promotion to Tape Drone II. My reinvention as a model prisoner had been a little too convincing. After a few minutes of awkwardness, Joe signed my release form. I left a week later.

7

THE THEORY
OF EVOLUTION

The new shipper/receiver gig was like a karmic gift from the wage slave gods for having survived computer prison. My day was split between the two Digitrex buildings. In the morning I'd hang out with Al, drinking coffee, eating pastries and reading every daily newspaper we could get our hands on (hey, 'the Journal' says textile orders are down). After lunch, I'd wander across the street to the other building and repeat the same basic formula with Leo.

Since these were office buildings and not a manufacturing operation, the concept of shipping and receiving was
a lot different. Instead of using fork trucks to haul pallets
of computer manuals, we just walked around the building
handing out FedEx envelopes and assorted small packages,
all the while making small talk with our favorite secretaries. We did this twice a day for an hour. No one ever questioned why it took two of us to deliver an envelope.

Whenever we weren't making deliveries, we'd hang around the office and wait for the various truckers and delivery types to ring the buzzer on the dock door. We never knew who would show up. Would it be the punch-drunk van driver haulin' toilet tissue? Maybe the tattooed snack cake guy with anger issues? Our favorite was Kicker, a whiskey-soaked garden gnome with the demeanor of an agitated ferret and an abiding appreciation for big gals.

Blessed with plenty of free time, Al and I set about turning our spacious office into a swingin' lounge, complete with Tiki lights and surround-sound mood enhancement. It was like working in the cage all over again, only this was bigger and better. Before long, our office became a sanctuary for white-collar types looking to escape the stress of their high-paying corporate positions. They used to say they wanted to trade jobs with us. They were only half-joking.

Al prided himself on his punctuality. He was convinced that if he came in late or took a sick day, he'd risk losing his cushy gig. So I was a little concerned the morning that I strolled in late and found his chair vacant and a red message light blinking on the office phone. It was Al, calling in sick to his own phone. Apparently, he'd injured his back in a freak shower mishap. He was ordered to lie still for three weeks. It was now up to me to do nothing all by myself.

Working by myself meant I had more interaction with the masses. While this was generally not advised, it did allow me to get to know one of the temp secretaries I'd noticed around the building. She was cute, funny, smart, worlds away from the archetypal office gal. After a few encounters (including a fax machine lesson rife with ulterior motives), I summoned up the nerve to ask her to lunch. Nearly two decades later we remain each other's main squeeze.

When AI returned to the roost, everything fell back into place. In a way, we knew we were actively living the good ol' days. We'd often remark on our good fortune, agreeing that we would gladly sign a contract consigning us to these jobs for the rest of our lives. Of course, in retrospect, this was just classic foreshadowing. Unbeknownst to us, the bottom was dropping out of Digitrex's bottom line. Somewhere off in a corporate boardroom plans were being made to dismantle our playhouse.

Part of Digitrex's allure was its "no layoff" policy — a rather noble refusal to throw its employees to the sharks during times of fiscal uncertainty. These good intentions went out the window when the company stock lost most of its value during a particularly wild stock market plunge. A month later, the company unveiled the Voluntary Disengagement Program, wherein Digitrex agreed to give employees a lump sum payment if they would agree to quit their jobs and not come back.

It was strongly implied that the offer (approximately three months of salary) would not be repeated and that future "buy-outs" would either be smaller in value or increasingly unpleasant in other unspecified terms. In other words, have the decency to quit now so we don't have to fire your sorry ass later. The pitch struck me as a bluff, designed to play on the fear and greed sectors of the brain. After a review of my marketable skills, I decided to call their bluff and stay in the game.

The corporate boys weren't joking when they said later versions of the VDP (commonly referred to as "the package") would be less attractive. The voluntary aspect was the first thing to go, quickly followed by a "re-thinking of the pay-out formula." By the time the right-sizing and blood-letting ended years later, "impacted" employees were receiving the rough equivalent of a Happy Meal coupon and a smack on the back of the head in exchange for their years of faithful service.

My carefree days as a shipper/receiver were coming to an end. If I wanted to ride the Digitrex bull as long as possible, I had to make a move. Logic dictated that the company would feed on the lowest members of the food chain first. I didn't need to see an organizational chart to realize that was me. To survive, I had to find a way to ascend at least one more rung on the corporate ladder. I decided to look for the office-based equivalent of moving boxes around.

I began to scan the Digitrex online job listing in search of a ticket out of Shangri-La. It always seemed to be the same mix of positions I was clearly unqualified for and more attainable gigs that sounded like chain gang details. Adding to the difficulty rating was that most hiring managers in the white-collar world equated shipper/receivers with trained chimps. The prospect of hiring one to live and work in the land of the carpeted cubicle was all but unthinkable.

After weeks of staring into the void and seeing only hot dog truck franchises staring back, I noticed that a Digitrex training department was looking for a technical seminar coordinator. I had no idea what that meant, but the office was only a mile from my apartment. The downside was that the group's manager had a horrible reputation. The rumor was that everyone who worked in the group was either trying to claw their way out or had been turned into a slack-jawed zombie.

It was a good horror story, but I was undeterred. I couldn't afford the luxury of looking for the perfect job, or even one without zombies. It was survival time. I needed to adapt, evolve, deceive! I spent the next two days trying to craft a suitable resume. I turned to the thesaurus, trying to find respectable sounding ways to describe my blue-collar activities. Box schlepping became "asset dispersal." Chatting up secretaries was recast as "timely and effective communication."

I submitted my resume and waited. After a week, I called the human resource department and asked about the status of my application. They liked my resume, but they were concerned that the "office environment" would not be a "good fit." It wasn't difficult to crack that code. They thought I was a chimp. I needed to convince them that my evolutionary progress was equal to their own. So I whipped a few complete sentences on them until they agreed to interview me.

I arrived for my interview in chinos and a sport coat, my long hair sculpted into a tasteful topiary. As with past interviews, I had once again transformed myself into someone I barely recognized so I could better explain who I was. The interview itself turned into a marathon interrogation session. I spoke to six or seven different members of the group. Each of them brought me a fresh cup of coffee. Before long I was visibly vibrating and speaking in tongues.

As I understood it, the object of an interview was to crea-tively lie about your past, shamelessly parrot the other par-ty's every utterance, and do it all with a smile. So I swal-lowed what was left of my pride and sold them the used Buick that was my soul. Everyone I talked to expressed concern that I wouldn't like the job. They were trying to scare me off. I would have none of it. I just tap-danced faster and faster. Oddly enough, the only person I didn't talk to was the group's manager.

The job itself sounded relatively harmless, but I had nothing to compare it to. Instead of moving boxes, I just assumed I'd be shuffling paper. Instead of talking to truckers, I pictured myself at the water cooler schmoozing office types. Despite everyone's concern for my wellbeing, I was certain I could survive breathing the rarefied office air. And after all, I didn't have much choice. Time was running out. The party was over, the beer was gone and the sun was coming up.

Days went by without an answer. I decided to take mat-
ters into my own hands and called Delores, the woman in
charge of the seminar series. She sounded upbeat. The
consenus was that I'd be perfect for the job. (Insert awk-
ward silence.) But they were still worried that I wouldn't
like the work. She asked if I wanted to try it for a day to
see if it was a "good fit." All this good fit crap was getting
on my nerves. I told her I was thrilled with the screwy job
and didn't need to take a test-drive.

Telling her that I was excited about the job was just more high-density bullshit. But somehow my display of conviction (no matter how disingenuous) sealed the deal. The next day I received the magic call offering me the job. There was no question that I would say yes — I needed this job. Still, the moment was bittersweet. I took a minute to look around. Somehow I knew that work — that life for that matter — would never be this uncomplicated again.

8

NEXT STOP, CUBE LAND

My first day on the job was both uneventful and odd. As a shipper/receiver, I could wander at will. Now there was a cube with my name on it, so that's where I stayed — for eight hours. I passed the time by adjusting and readjusting the desk accessories (stapler Feng Shui) and by talking quietly on the phone so that no one could hear me. My co-workers reinforced my paranoia by tiptoeing around me like I was a smelly gorilla who had materialized in their midst.

After a few days of hiding out in my cube, I worked up the nerve to forage for snack food and companionship. My new coworkers appeared to be a congenial bunch, yet something wasn't quite right. No one seemed to like their job and no one was comfortable expressing that opinion. I wondered what could be the cause of all this dissatisfaction and paranoia. It didn't take long for me to find out. It was Friday morning — time for the weekly staff meeting.

We took our seats in the conference room and waited in near-silence. Finally, the door swung open and in walked the source of everyone's misery. It was Marge, the group's manager, a dough-faced demon with a Moe Howard haircut. She launched into a rambling diatribe that was equal parts paranoia and thinly-veiled threat. I felt like I was watching *The Guyana Massacre* with Marge cast as Rev. Jim Jones. After an hour, I was ready for the Kool Aid.

As we filed out of the conference room, I looked around for a sign that what I'd witnessed was some sort of initiation rite. Instead, the consensus was that this was just a routine staff meeting, and that if anything Marge was more subdued than usual. I didn't know what to say. All I knew for certain was that a crazy person had stolen an hour of my life. I asked the other group members for advice. They just rolled their eyes and said, "You'll get used to it."

I was the technical seminar cabin boy. My job was to assist Delores by helping her schedule the visiting seminar speakers (a medley of crackpot academics) and then act as their personal gopher on the day of the seminar. The main problem was that Delores, despite her good-natured demeanor and impeccable taste in cardigan sweaters, was basically useless. It was like working with your grandmother. Only without the prospect of homemade apple pie.

I had imagined office life as a series of long lunches punctuated by chitchat around the copier. It wasn't long before the Faustian bargain became apparent. When I worked in the warehouse, no one cared what I said, so I said whatever I wanted. But in cube land, a big part of the job was protecting your perceived position on the corporate ladder. As a result, no one ever said what they thought. Instead, they'd go to meetings and say what they thought the person above them wanted to hear.

I began to wonder if all office jobs were the same. Then I met Kevin, the videographer in charge of taping the technical seminars. He seemed to be enjoying himself, so I asked what life was like in his group, the division's communication department. According to Kevin, the group was wildly dysfunctional in its own way, but it was a mostly stress-free form of dysfunction. That sounded good to me, so I started maneuvering for a department transfer.

A few weeks later I got word that the communication group was looking to hire someone to edit the division's newsletter. Kevin paved the way for the interview and a week later I was hired. Marge was beside herself. I couldn't have been happier. Instead of attending marathon meetings, I hung out in my new cube listening to music and writing newsletter articles (business updates and blood drives). At lunch, Kevin and I would go to my house and drink beer.

In a lot of ways, this new job reminded me of my care-free days working with Al and Leo. Given my track record, I should have recognized this tranquility for what it was — more foreshadowing. Digitrex was still on the fiscal downslide. Layoffs were rampant and the "re-orgs" were coming fast and furious. All this uncertainty came to a head when it was announced that our division had been sold to Outcome, a monolithic California-based semiconductor company.

The new regime changed everything. Once the deal was signed, meetings were hastily scheduled to indoctrinate workers into the Outcome corporate culture. Photo IDs (worn around the neck, no less) were mandatory. Security checkpoints were set up throughout the building. It was Fascism 101 and the result was equally textbook. The weak turned on the weaker to show worthiness. Latent troublemakers (yours truly) joined up with the resistance.

Our group was disbanded. We were told we were now "technical writers." Instead of goofing around, we were forced to dress up in clean suits ("bunny suits") and spend all day in the fabrication lab, witnessing the tedium of semi-conductor chip manufacture. Ostensibly, this was because we were going to be writing technical manuals. In truth it was just a charade intended to scare us away. No layoff equals no severance check. They don't call it evil genius for nothing.

A few weeks after the coup, I noticed an ad in the Sunday paper. A software company called GearTech was looking for a communications writer. The job seemed like a bit of a stretch, but since I had experience as a newsletter editor and a technical writer (ahem), I figured it was worth a shot. The ad played up the company's "work hard, play hard" philosophy, promising a game room, movie passes and other goodies. The ad worked. I submitted my resume.

I was excited when I got a call from GearTech inviting me in for an interview. But when I showed up, I didn't detect any of the advertised good times. Instead, I was promptly ushered into a conference room where I was interrogated by various "gears" (the actual name for employees), given a writing test, forced to produce a handwriting sample for "analysis" and shown a video starring Dr. Dave, GearTech's high-profile CEO. I was there for five hours.

I had no expectation that I'd ever hear back from GearTech. Then I got a call from Brenda, the HR servo-robot in charge of recruiting gears. My tests had come back positive. They wanted me. As much as I had been thoroughly spooked by the interview/internment session, I couldn't face the prospect of being trapped in the bunny suit one more day. Plus, GearTech was offering more money. I threw better judgment to the wind and agreed to join Dr. Dave's army.

As expected, GearTech was not the party portrayed in the pamphlet. The first thing I noticed was the silence. As I sat in my cube, I couldn't detect any conversation, laughter or audible sign of human interaction — just the sound of fingers tapping quietly on keyboards. The only exception was when I'd come across a small grouping of gears whispering to each other in a neighboring cube. As I passed by they would look up and immediately stop talking. Not good.

While the vibe tended toward high tech ghost town, a constant effort was made to massage gear morale. The biggest extravaganza of the year took place on Halloween, when all gears were strongly encouraged to don costumes. (I opted for a homemade "alien invasion" jumpsuit complete with plastic Devo pompadour.) But for every perk there was a quirk. For example, Dr. Dave hated cigarettes, so gears were not allowed to smoke — even at home.

I was responsible for writing scripts for employee meetings. One recurring event was a question and answer session called "Ask Dr. Dave." It went like this: When no one was looking, gears would drop questions into suggestion boxes set up throughout the building. I'd retrieve the scrawled queries and help write the official responses. Dr. Dave would read the questions and answers verbatim from index cards, while gears looked on in disbelieving silence.

According to my contacts in human resources, new gears either fled right away or allowed their brain chemistry to be altered and stayed forever. I started to look for a way out. The Internet boom was in full swing and a Web gig seemed like it might be a suitable next step. Internet companies were popping up every 5 minutes, so finding a job was easy. I interviewed with a startup called Roxy.com and landed a gig as a copywriter. Goodbye, Dr. Dave!

Much has been written about the Internet gold rush of the late 90s. When I made the move to dot-com world, the hysteria was still in effect. Thousands of new companies — flush with investment bucks and dubious business plans (let's sell cat food online!) — were defining a new industry by default. Busloads of techies were needed to work the pulleys and levers. I went from writing corp speak to "providing content" and never looked back. Click here to learn more.

Roxy.com was a fledgling consumer electronics "e-tailer" run by two brothers, Bob and Mitch. Bob was the brains of the outfit, a classic type A personality. Mitch was Bob's brother and that's where his qualifications ended. My gig was working in the "Web World" pen at the back of the rented office space, churning out cheesy copy for banner ads and product catalog descriptions. Like the rest of my dot-com contemporaries, I was doing stuff I had no idea how to do, as quickly as possible.

Like ninety percent of the other Internet companies that started around this time, Roxy was burning money at a furious clip. But it couldn't last forever. Once the millennium clock struck 2001, the drugs began to wear off. Sales slumped, suppliers grew tired of chasing checks and the venture capitalists who fed the frenzy stopped returning calls. The layoffs started in earnest and those of us lucky enough to stick around stopped working altogether.

Days before Roxy closed its doors, I got a call from a re-cruiter at Lycos, one of the few Web outfits with a future not being measured in hours. After working for only six months on the Internet railroad I was considered experi-enced and my "content" was in demand. The vibe at the Lycos interview was positive, the job seemed like it had potential and I was days away from being unemployed. When they offered me a writer gig, I agreed on the spot.

In the beginning, Lycos was an enjoyable ride. My coworkers were a smart and funny bunch, and because worker demand was still running ahead of supply, management stayed out of the way. It was as if the geeks had inherited one fertile corner of the earth and a new social order was in play. Everyone came and went as they wanted; "business casual" was a Ramones t-shirt and bunny slippers; and meetings dissolved into debates over *Star Wars* trivia.

If my previous work experience taught me anything it was that job happiness is an inherently unstable compound. Lycos was no different. A year after I started, the company's founder sold the business to a shady foreign conglomerate. Out went the creative types who started and nurtured the company. In came the bean counters in blue shirts. The bloodletting began immediately. Massive layoffs, one after another, gutted the staff and spiked the underlying paranoia.

The layoffs always went down the same way. On Black Friday (always a Friday, the date always leaked in advance), management would wander up and down the aisles like grim reapers, pausing at their victims' cubes to whisper the three words we came to dread: "Got a minute?" At that point, there was no escape. You were ushered into a room, handed papers to sign and a cardboard box for personal items. Ten minutes later you were out on the street, processed and unemployed.

I managed to avoid the first major layoff, but not the second. And while I knew full well that the law of averages was bound to catch up with me, getting the tap on the shoulder still turned out to be an emotional, fucked-up experience. I think I actually hugged a few people on my way out the door. It was weird sitting in my car next to a cardboard box filled with the ephemeral crap from my cube. Over three decades of employment leading up to this one solitary impossibly-dumb moment. Is that all there is?

Yes, that's all there is. Which makes it harder to admit there is no moral to this story, no Hollywood ending, no recognizable picture when you connect the dots. If there is a point, it's that there is no point. Except that maybe having a job gives life structure — something reliable to conform to and rebel against. Take it away and all you're left with is the taunt of endless possibility and unpaid cable bills. But that's me. You could have a better theory. If so, let's hear it. I've got plenty of time.

OFF THE CLOCK

When you start a new job, you look around at the cast of characters and wonder . . . who is cool, who is crazed, who will I have a beer with after work? If you're lucky, a few of your coworkers will transcend that title, become friends and stick around after the job is done. Overtime thanks to Scott, Rich, Craig, Al, Leo, Jeff, Kevin (summit!), Jamie, Todd, et al.

Deluxe combo platter thanks to Dorothea, for deep connection, creative inspiration and backward proofing at 30,000 feet. (If you ever need another fax lesson, just say the word.) Monster-sized thanks to Kerry Testa for wrapping these misadventures in such a cool cover.

Finally, credit where credit is due to Harvey Pekar. Discovering his sublime autobiographical work in *American Splendor* in the 80s surely planted the seed that grew into this unwieldy vine. Hats off to Harvey.

— Stephen Beaupre

40 Hour Man is one of those fortunate projects that grew organically, over time, subject only to its own peculiar (and charmed) internal logic. Of course, certain individuals were waiting along the crooked pathway to lend a hand when needed.

Thanks to my wife Serena for backing me up foursquare in my artistic endeavors, and indeed for the shared undertaking of adventures way beyond what we could have imagined for ourselves. I'll also say, she has taught me a thing or two about the art of the narrative, proving that you can indeed teach an old dog new tricks!

I am also grateful to several colleagues in the comix biz who have opined to me that *40 Hour Man* is **funny**. That is a darn big word — high praise indeed from one's peers in this game. J.R. Williams in particular comes to mind as a supporter. Brett Warnock not only observed that the book had a great "hook," but advised on book design, enhancing in no small measure this very item you hold in your hands.

— Steve Lafler